Heart Scars

Heart Scars

Elaine Gasper-Adams

I would like to dedicate this book to my children Jolene, Joshua, Justin and my grandchildren. You all are my reason for living, I could not imagine my life without y'all. Thank you for loving me through my mess, you are my greatest blessings.

I love y'all with all that I am.

Also want to say thank you for all the love and encouragement from family and friends who support me. I love y'all too.

Special thanks to Erika for the idea and encouragement to write this book. Love you big, Cousin.

My Grandchildren

The beauty in your eyes

Could light up the skies

I'd walk for miles and miles

Just to see your sweet smiles

Those precious little laughs

It's like music I must have

The joy of watching you grow

Makes my heart overflow

Those chubby little fingers

Wrapped around my hand

It's almost more than I can stand

Your tiny hearts have so much love to give

You're what gives me the strength to live

The greatest gift I've ever been given

Is to have y'all as my grandchildren.

Table of Contents

My Story..1

The Cry of a Child..5

Be Silent...6

Broken Pieces...8

Fake a Smile..10

Addiction...12

Love Just Isn't Enough...13

Stab Me in the Back...14

The Devil You Know...16

Searching for the Light..18

Sweet Amber Fire...19

Betrayal...21

Daring to Hope...22

How Savvy is the Devil...23

What Will Be...24

The Devil is a Liar...25

Why..26

Need a Friend..27

Set Free..28

The Reckoning...29

No Longer..30

Whispered Lies..32

You Promised...33

Good Girl...34

Single Mother..35

Undefiled...37

The Night...39

Love Is...40

Just a part of my story:

Life has not always dealt me the greatest of hands. My life has not been all bad let me say that. There have been some wonderful times. But like most people there have been a lot of traumas. I've gone through a lot of things as a child that not everyone has gone through. I do understand there are people that have had a lot harder life than I have. This is just part of my story and some of the things I have been through. I was born to parents who have struggled with addiction their whole life. I also have Chiari Malformation, which is a condition that caused my brain stem to go down into my spinal cord. They didn't know what it was when I was a child. But it affected me very much. I was paralyzed and in the hospital at the age of three for a little while. I was fortunate that I had my grandmother and my Aunt Jo that took turns staying with me. Then one day I was just able to move again. A lot of things happened as I was growing up. I was sexually assaulted and was molested but I never told anyone about being molested until I was older and had kids of my own. It's not something I've ever really been able to talk about. It's something I still deal with that causes me issues, but I know I will be ok one day. Now on to the main things this book is about. My life being married to an addict who did a lot of things to hurt me in his addiction.

It's hard to imagine what kind of man would have has his wife befriend women just so he can make it look normal for these women to be coming around. But then again, it's hard to imagine what kind of women befriend a man's wife just so it looks normal for them to be coming around. All these women had an addiction that had a hold on them. I seen their addiction and tried to be a friend and speak life into them. Little did I know, every one of those women and my husband were spreading death into my marriage and my family. That evil demon called addiction allowed all of them to commit adultery together. They all knew me or about me and our family but had not one once of apathy. They even went as far as to cheat together while I lay sleeping in the other room resting for work the next day. I know I look like a fool for not seeing all of this but, it's amazing what your mind will allow you to go through when it has taught you how to protect yourself from a life of trauma. That flight, fight, fawn, or freeze is a very real thing. I have at one time, or another experienced every one of these as a response to trauma in my life and in my marriage.

The fawn was my first stage, pretending not to see the things he was doing. Next was the freeze, the depression, just shutting down and not wanting to do anything at all. Then came the fight, I got angrier with every instance I found out about.

I wanted to fight not only the women, but my husband as well. Then came the final stage for me, finally the flight.

I caught him at the river with the woman he cheated on me with for five years. The one I hated the most. So, when he left one night I packed some things, and I left. It was then that I decided I was never going back. Now it's taken me years to culminate all these poems that just poured out my heartache and my struggle. They are very personal and raw.

I pray that in some way they can help someone else know that they are not alone in their mess and struggle. I also hope they give someone a little bit of strength to keep going every day when they don't feel like they can and to walk away if they need to. Don't give in to the darkness.

The Cry of a Child

I only ever wanted to feel love

Instead, I had to learn to be tough

Even as a child my life was rough

All my dreams beaten down and crushed

Being shuffled around from place to place

As a kid it's hard to face

The ones who are supposed to protect you

Are the very ones destroying you

They are too busy chasing that high

To even hear you cry

The cry of a 3-year-old child

One that should be up running around wild

Instead laid there paralyzed

Parents who were not by your side

The entire time you were hospitalized

Laying there scared, not understanding what I'd done wrong

Trying so hard just to stay strong.

Be Silent

Why does he not stop
Can he not hear me cry
As I lay there with him atop
All the while asking why
Hands that don't belong there
Eyes only a blank stare
Mind trying to shut down
Praying just to be found
Begging for him to just relent
But threats keep me silent
You turn for help only to be accused
So, you just continue to be abused
Your body no longer your own
The secret forever keeping you alone

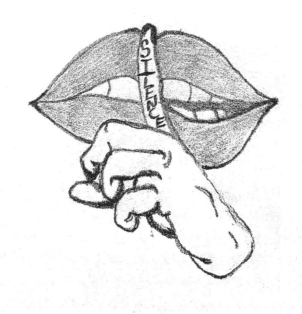

Broken Pieces

Broken and crushed from the beginning

All this hurt keeps my head spinning

So much emotion filled to the brim

So real I could reach out and touch them

For the sins I've committed I've tried to atone

Still, I feel so utterly alone

This bitterness grows like a cancer

I cry out but hear no answer

Lost and lonely like a little lamb

I smile though it feels like a scam

I can't handle this lonely feeling

Wish I knew how to start this healing

The weight of our problems rest on my shoulders

I need some help hurling these giant boulders

I cannot do this on my own

This road was not meant to walk alone

Hand in hand, side by side

Elaine Gasper-Adams

We should not fear the coming tide

We said we'd face this world together

You and me always and forever

We came into this with both a shattered soul

Thinking we could make each other whole

Know matter what I do

I don't feel I'm enough for you

My broken pieces jagged like a knife

Piercing and wounding your life

Please forgive the pain I've brought

It was only love that I sought.

Fake A Smile

So afraid to speak these feelings

So afraid to make a move

I know I'm not helping with this healing

If nothing changes nothing will improve

I find the tools of production

I find the evil hidden dope

I pretend I don't see the destruction

Feeling it's the only way to cope

This sea of lies is taking me under

The waves crashing down

Tearing me asunder

This ripping and roaring

The anxiety so real

I fake a smile

So no one knows how I feel

For twenty years I've prayed

He would break his addiction

Mind and soul numb

I pray now with more conviction

My mind is aching

My heart is breaking

This disease is crushing

Laying out souls for the taking

Night sweats and fearful screams

Waking from these horrific dreams

Heart pounding, pulse racing

Evil demons forever chasing

Stealing the spark and wondrous joy

From this once loving playful boy

I've tried to be his relief

To be his rescue

Sadly, I've come to realize

There's nothing I can do

So, for me I'll have to heal

I'll have to mend

Or for the both of us

It could forever be the end

Addiction

The light in your eyes

Began to slowly dim over time

The darkness taking hold

Like a demon so evil and bold

You speak in riddles

Your words meaning so little

Tongue dripping with sweet lies

We've given this too many tries

I can't shake this horrible feeling

If I don't escape now, I'll never find healing

I've been drowning in your world for years

With no one to hear me or see the tears

Pain so vast like a never-ending ocean

An encompassing vortex of emotion

Love Just Isn't Enough

How do you rest when your soul is weary?

When your mind is lost, and your body feels dreary

You wonder where the years went

Was it time well spent?

Or did you stay because you felt stuck

Like you're gasping for air drowning in the muck

You wonder should you leave

But you don't want to grieve

For the love that is lost

And all that its cost

It takes strength to sever ties

Will it happen now because of lies

So many times, you turned the other cheek

But you're tired of being mousy and meek

Time to stand and be tough

Sometimes love just isn't enough.

Stab Me in the Back

Friends, but how could that be

You stabbed me in the back hoping I wouldn't see

Taking advantage of the hand reaching out

Downplaying my sense of doubt

I watched your struggle with addiction

You'd hug me and talk about your affliction

I was the friend I seen you needed

Ignoring the warnings I should've headed

Pretending to be the shoulder I too was looking for

Just so you could get your foot in the door

You say that it was all unplanned

Befriending me just to sleep with my husband

Yall say it was the drugs that made you that way

But that doesn't make the pain go away

Somehow that makes it harder to feel

I pray one day I find the strength to heal.

The Devil You Know

Sometimes your choices are slim

You don't get to choose him or him

You lay down with the devil you know

Or you spend your time being alone

That knight and shining armor doesn't exist

He'll come as everything you can't resist

You'll think you found the one

Only to realize he's a loaded gun

He'll marry you and make you his wife

Then he'll slowly destroy your life

Next, you're screaming and out of control

You don't see the damage taking its toll

You feel yourself starting to slip away

You turn to leave, and he begs you to stay

He says just give us one more try

You stay but you slowly die inside.

Searching for The Light

When darkness lurks in every corner of your mind

You search for the light you just can't seem to find

You struggle everyday just to get out of bed

The voices never ceasing in your head

Telling you, you don't deserve to live

But you know you have so much more to give

The life you dare to hope for

You thought you had but now you're not so sure

All the emotions you've been feeling

All those dreams you were dreaming

Seem to scatter to the wind

The loneliness starting to descend.

Sweet Amber Fire

The whiskey blurs the image I see in the mirror

Wiping the tears, I still can't see any clearer

Drowning in that sweet amber fire

Letting it take me higher and higher

Trying desperately to kill a lifetime of heartbreak

Wishing all the pain would just dissipate.

Betrayal

How dare you even say you love me

When I see betrayal in every woman's face I see

Just when I think I'm starting to heal

More pain comes and I no longer wanna feel

Wanting to numb this hurt

But I know that's not what I need to do

Because that would make me no better than you.

Daring To Hope

This life is so full of sorrow

Daring to hope for a better tomorrow

It only brings disappointment and pain

Drowning in this acidic rain

I used to believe in true love

That there was one for me from above

Living with a man with secrets and lies

Makes me realize I must cut ties

My hearts been breaking for so long

Thinking it was destiny, but I was so wrong

All I ever wanted was to be the only one

Now my heart screams run girl run.

How Savvy Is the Devil

I've always tried to be a people pleaser

Not realizing the reason was so much deeper

Someone once told me life's too short to be unhappy

Until that moment I never grasped how the devil was so savvy

That hand of darkness creeping to take hold

Those shadowy fingers reaching for my soul

The demons working to extinguish my light

Seeking to suppress my ability to fight

Pretending to be OK knowing I was miserable

Praying everyday just to be invisible

My existence filled with so much drama

Struggling to escape a life full of trauma.

What Will Be

You say I'm your only one

That our love is not done

But you took parts of me

That now no one will ever see

All the promises you made

The love we had only fades

You tore pieces from my soul

What's left now is a deep dark hole

From that darkness I try to crawl

I pull my way up only to fall

You turned my life into chaos

Now our family is so lost

Our lives are in such a whirlwind

But I say no more, this disaster must end

I built a wall around my heart

Somehow, I'll make a new start

Through Christ who strengthens me

For only He knows what will be.

The Devil Is a Liar

The tears streaming down your face

What is the darkness of this place

You pray to see just a glimmer of light

Something doesn't feel right

You feel the prickle of warning go up your spine

You tell yourself everything is fine

But that eerie feeling just won't go away

Something is telling you not to stay

You try to move but your legs are frozen

Try to scream but your voice feels broken

You hear their murmurs whisper in your ear

"Your demons like to play with you here"

They want to keep you trapped in your fear

They hate the light in you that shines so bright

They fear the lioness in you willing to fight

You gotta know that devil is a liar

So, light that spark into a raging fire.

Why

Why do people hurt you so much

They lie, and cheat and steal your soul

They say it's your heart they want to touch

But it's only your body they want to hold

They take and take until they suck you dry

You give and give until you're dead inside

You try so hard to come back to life

But it's a slow and steady stride

You're torn between the life you had and the one you envisioned

Funny how the past can keep you imprisoned.

Elaine Gasper-Adams

Need a Friend

Fighting the darkness that tears at my soul
The blackness, the emptiness that continues to grow
The life I had built crashing around me
How is this the person I've come to be
The love that once existed shattered to the wind
I can't stand this loneliness, I just need a friend
Someone who makes my soul feel protected
I'm tired of being scared and so rejected
But life has a funny way of turning around
When you're lost and feeling low down
You thought you had it right off the rift
But life just kind of flipped the script
All the things you thought you knew
 Seem to be backwards, through and through
When your heart goes to battle with your mind
 You gotta leave everything else behind.

Set Free

There's a hole where your love used to be

You destroyed the best part of me

You took my love for granted

You ran and left me here stranded

The thoughts of you keep me paralyzed

Our lives were so intertwined

The betrayal plays like a nightmare in my mind

I need to break free of these chains that bind

I'm starting to see my worth now

I know I will get through this somehow

Through the strength the Lord gives me

One day I will be set free.

The Reckoning

Minds are aching

Hearts are breaking

Thoughts are racing

Feet are pacing

Sorrow comes creeping

Soul is grieving

This pain is crushing

Body is numbing

Only time will tell

If we come out of this hell

The silence is deafening

It's time for the reckoning.

No Longer

Being alone is so very hard

It's not the loneliness that's the problem

It's being alone with your broken heart

It's knowing this is all because of him

The memories that cut like a knife

All you ever wanted was to be his wife

His words would wrap you up in a sweet embrace

But the truth was like a shattering slap in the face

Losing all the love that was built

Knowing all that's left now is guilt

Guilt of a life that could've been

Having flashbacks of way back when

Back when our love was still new

But then reality breaks through

You're left to sort through what life has become

Knowing your old life is just done

You must move on but don't know how

It's time to realize who you are now

You are a warrior who will only get stronger

You are powerful and helpless no longer.

Whispered Lies

They say time heals everything

So why do I still feel every sting

I hate you for destroying me

Not even in my nightmares did I think this is where we'd be

What a beautiful love we once shared

But that all shattered when you showed me you no longer cared

I used to believe we were made for each other

That for either of us there was no other

I pictured us growing old side by side

Instead, I found out you just lied

Every whispered promise was a lie

Every memory now only makes me cry

You were supposed to be my forever

But all the destruction you caused shows me you're my never

 Never again will I allow you to hurt me

Because I am now and forever free.

You Promised

You say my head was made for your chest

That your arms were a place I could rest

The way you caressed my hair in your sleep

You swore you were mine for always to keep

You promised that I was safe with you

That there was nothing you wouldn't do

You said you would protect my heart for all time

To hold me until the sun refused to shine

I want with all my soul for this to be true

But my mind is confused, and I don't know what to do

Cause even though you told me I was your whole world

I still found you talking to all those other girls

I don't know if we'll make it another day

For in a moment of weakness you threw it all away.

A Good Girl

You say you want a good girl

Until she wants to love the whole world

Talk about wanting joyful bliss

But can't even show a little forgiveness

You tell me you're doing all you can

But you can't even except me for who I am

You use my compassion as a reason to be mad at me

But it's a big part of who I'll always be

Wishing harm on someone else is insane

I don't want to be the reason for another person's pain

I will not apologize for having a big heart

I think that's what will end up keeping us apart

Elaine Gasper-Adams

Single Mother

Life was not supposed to be this way

It's a struggle every single day

I never planned on being a single mother

But then again neither did any of the others

Now I feel like I gotta rob Peter just to pay Paul

Waiting on that miracle call

Hoping for that job you so desperately need

Knowing you have mouths to feed

You cry softly at night, so your kids don't hear

Affecting their little minds is now your biggest fear.

Undefiled

I stare up at the midnight sky

Watching the embers of the fire fly

Feeling the soft breeze blow across my face

Dreaming about some far-off place

The beat of my heart matching that of a whip-poor-will

The light of the fireflies gives me a little thrill

I sigh as the rain starts to gently fall

I hear a distant coyote call

I think back to being a small child

Running free and feeling so wild

I laid back, closed my eyes and smiled

The sweetness of that little girl so undefiled

What I wouldn't give to go back and protect her

From all the things she had to endure

She was so innocent, so pure

But those things have only made her stronger

For they just taught her how to conquer.

The Night

She felt the wind blowing through her hair

Lifting her face without a care

That bright blue moon kissing the sky

She raises her arms wishing she could fly

Riding down her favorite back roads

In her old truck faster and faster she goes

She glides down the highway climbing the mountain

Stopping only to drink from that crystal fountain

She's on a high only music can take you

Her playlist knowing what her hearts going through

All her life she's had to fight

Those stars holding the secrets of the night

Now she no longer feels so lonesome

Cause something about the night gives her freedom.

Love Is

Love is not a battlefield
It's supposed to be what heals
Love shouldn't cost you everything
It should be what makes your heart sing
It's not jealous or boastful
It's the thing that makes you hopeful
Love is joy and happiness
It's not crazy and stress
Love is not temporary and fleeting
It's what keeps your heart beating
It's cherishing the person you adore
And everything worth fighting for.

Elaine Gasper-Adams is a mother of three and a grandmother of four. For the last 9 years she has been a devoted school bus driver. She has been writing poetry since she was 15 years old. Over the last six years she has gone through a lot of traumas. It was hard for her to pull herself out of the darkness of that trauma but through writing she has found an outlet of sorts. Writing poetry is like a form of therapy for her. She hopes that her words may inspire other people to know that they are not alone. Elainegasper.adams@gmail.com

Elaine Gasper-Adams

Made in the USA
Columbia, SC
27 April 2025